AMAZING ANIMALS

BEAVERS

BY KATE RIGGS

HIGHLAND PARK PUBLIC LIBRARY
494 LAUREL AVE.
HIGHLAND PARK, IL 60035-2690
847-432-0215

CREATIVE EDUCATION • CREATIVE PAPERBACKS

Beavers are **rodents**. There are two kinds of beavers. One kind lives in North America. The other kind lives in Europe and Asia. Beavers live in wooded places near water.

rodents animals, like rats and mice, that have sharp front teeth, hair or fur, and feed their babies with milk

A beaver's tail is long and flat. Its teeth are strong and sharp. A beaver uses its teeth to break branches and trees. Then it builds a dam to make a pond.

Beavers like to chew trees with soft bark, such as birch

Beavers weigh 30 to 70 pounds (13.6–31.8 kg). North American beavers are the second-largest rodents in the world. Their coats can be light brown to black in color.

North American beavers are 35 to 40 inches (89–102 cm) long

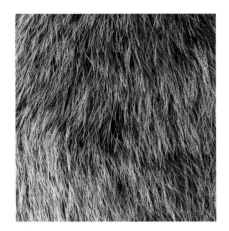

A beaver's fur is waterproof because beavers swim a lot. The two back paws are webbed. This helps beavers move through water. Beavers can swim at speeds of up to five miles (8 km) per hour.

Beavers use comb claws on their back feet to clean fur

Beavers eat wood and plants. They grip wood with their front claws. Beavers eat wood and bark from any kind of tree. They eat grassy plants like cattails that grow in water, too.

Eurasian beavers have triangle-shaped openings in the nose

*A one-year-old beaver
kit is called a yearling*

A mother beaver has a **litter** of four to nine **kits**. Newborn kits have fur and front teeth. They can swim a day after they are born. They drink milk from their mother for up to three months.

kits baby beavers

litter a group of baby beavers

There are usually 4 to 12 beavers in a colony

Beaver families live together in groups called colonies. Their homes are in **lodges** or **dens**. Beaver kits live with their families for two and a half years. Then they start new families. Beavers can live more than 20 years.

dens homes that are hidden on a riverbank

lodges homes that are built in water out of sticks and mud

Beavers work together to build dams and homes. Beaver dams are usually 6 feet (1.8 m) high and 15 feet (4.6 m) long. The longest beaver dam is 2,790 feet (850 m)! It is more than 30 years old.

Mud is used to fill in spaces around sticks in a dam

People used to hunt beavers for their fur. Beavers almost disappeared. But now there are millions of beavers! People like to watch these busy animals at work!

A beaver's tongue keeps water out of its mouth as it works

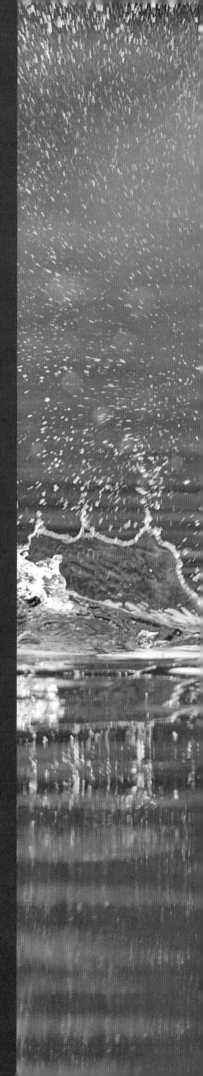

A Beaver Story

Why do beavers slap their tails on water? People in Florida told a story about this. Long ago, beavers built dams for people. But then some people stole kits to keep as pets. The beavers got upset. They chewed through the dams. The people's land flooded! Today, beavers slap their tails on the water whenever they see humans!

Read More

Clark, Carson, and Jim Clark. *The Adventures of Buddy the Beaver: Buddy Explores the Pond*. Johnson City, Tenn.: Mountain Trail Press, 2010.

Moore, Helen H. *Beavers*. Greenvale, N.Y.: Mondo, 1996.

Websites

Enchanted Learning: Beaver
http://www.enchantedlearning.com/subjects/mammals/rodent/Beavprintout.shtml
This site has facts about the beaver and a picture to color.

Wild Kratts: Build It Beaver
http://www.pbs.org/parents/wildkratts/episodes/season-1/
Watch a video about a beaver lodge.

Note: Every effort has been made to ensure that the websites listed above are suitable for children, that they have educational value, and that they contain no inappropriate material. However, because of the nature of the Internet, it is impossible to guarantee that these sites will remain active indefinitely or that their contents will not be altered.

BEAVERS

Published by Creative Education and
Creative Paperbacks
P.O. Box 227, Mankato, Minnesota 56002
Creative Education and Creative Paperbacks
are imprints of The Creative Company
www.thecreativecompany.us

Design by The Design Lab
Production by Chelsey Luther
Printed in the United States of America

Photographs by Alamy (Kevin Ebi, Robert McGouey/
Wildlife, Prisma Bildagentur AG), Biosphoto (Fabian
Bruggmann & Bruno Fouillat, Tom & Pat Leeson/
Ardea), Getty Images (Sven Zacek), iStockphoto
(webmink), National Geographic Creative (JOEL
SARTORE), Newscom (Bernd Zoller Image Broker),
Shutterstock (BMJ, dan_nurgitz, Bill Frische),
SuperStock (Ken Baehr/Alaska Stock-Design Pics,
Minden Pictures)

Copyright © 2015 Creative Education,
Creative Paperbacks
International copyright reserved in all countries. No
part of this book may be reproduced in any form
without written permission from the publisher.

Library of Congress Cataloging-in-Publication Data
Riggs, Kate.
Beavers / Kate Riggs.
p. cm. — (Amazing animals)
Summary: A basic exploration of the appearance,
behavior, and habitat of beavers, nature's swimming
engineers. Also included is a story from folklore
explaining why beavers slap their tails.
Includes index.
ISBN 978-1-60818-486-6 (hardcover)
ISBN 978-1-62832-086-2 (pbk)
1. Beavers—Juvenile literature. I. Title. II. Series:
Amazing animals.
QL737.R632R54 2015
599.37—dc23   2013051246

CCSS: RI.1.1, 2, 4, 5, 6, 7; RI.2.2, 5, 6, 7, 10;
RI.3.1, 5, 7, 8; RF.1.1, 3, 4; RF.2.3, 4

First Edition
9 8 7 6 5 4 3 2 1

JP
599.37
R569

JUN 2015   18.95

P9-BYB-223